"Blizzard in Khimki: A Moscow Survival Tale"

Sunil Kumar

Published by Sunil Kumar, 2024.

"BLIZZARD IN KHIMKI: A MOSCOW SURVIVAL TALE"

First edition. October 18, 2024.

Copyright © 2024 Sunil Kumar.

ISBN: 979-8227218919

Written by Sunil Kumar.

Introduction

I understood this was a typical Russian winter storm as the frigid wind howled through the streets of Khimki, a little city on Moscow's outskirts. I had no idea that the next three days would challenge human survival instincts and endurance, permanently altering my viewpoint on the unadulterated force of nature and the fortitude of the human spirit.

"Blizzard in Khimki: A Moscow Survival Tale" is an engross narrative of an unplanned adventure that happened during what was meant to be a regular business trip to Russia's capital. This book offers a first-hand view of the difficulties experienced by people caught in one of the most severe winter storms to strike the Moscow area in recent history, therefore guiding readers on a terrifying journey.

The narrative starts with my arrival in Moscow, a city with a rich past, breathtaking architecture, and hard winters. Having traveled often, I felt I was ready for whatever the Russian winter would provide. Nothing, though, could have equipped me for the ferocity of the snowfall that would sweep Khimki, turning a familiar metropolitan scene into a dangerous white wilderness.

This novel distinguishes itself from other survival tales by having a modern urban backdrop. Although many survival stories center on far-off wilderness environments, "Blizzard in Khimki" examines the difficulties of surviving a natural disaster in a heavily populated location, when the infrastructure and luxuries we sometimes take for granted suddenly becomes unreliable or inaccessible.

Readers will come across a number of important topics throughout the story that emphasize the complexity of urban survival and the human ability for adaptation: The frailty of modern urban living against severe weather disasters is one of the main subjects. We see as the blizzard gets stronger how rapidly a busy metropolis may be brought to a standstill with disrupted essential services, paralyzed transit systems, and swamped communication networks.

The book also looks at the need of community and cooperation during disaster. Strangers must join together, pooling their resources and knowledge, to raise their chances of survival while the storm rages on. This surprising friendship reminds us strongly of our shared humanity and the strength we can discover in unity—even in the most difficult conditions.

Examining how the human mind handles great stress, solitude, and uncertainty, the book also explores the psychological sides of survival. When confronted with life-threatening events, readers will learn about the mental methods and coping mechanisms that might make all the difference between hopelessness and resilience.

The vital need of preparedness and adaptation in survival situations forms a fourth essential theme. By means of my experiences and those of other stranded people, the book shows how even simple survival knowledge and improvisation techniques may be lifesaver when contemporary conveniences fail. Readers will learn useful survival skills ranging from locating cover and staying warm to controlling few food and water supplies, which would be quite helpful in many kinds of emergencies.

Written for a broad readership, "Blizzard in Khimki" appeals to adventure seekers, tourists, city people, and everyone else drawn in by true survival tales. For those who live in or visit places likely to experience extreme winter conditions as well as those who wish to be more ready for unanticipated events in metropolitan settings, it provides insightful analysis.

This book offers a vicarious delight for the adventure seeker so they may feel the urgency of a survival situation from the security of their homes. Travelers will get useful guidance on getting ready for and handling severe weather in foreign countries as well as understanding of the cultural facets of crisis management worldwide.

Those who live in cities, especially those in colder climes, will see the possible weaknesses of urban living and the need of personal readiness from a fresh angle. The book is a wake-up call, pushing readers to think about how they may handle should the infrastructure of their city fail during a natural disaster.

Furthermore, "Blizzard in Khimki" teaches everyone interested in crisis management and emergency readiness important skills. Examining the choices chosen and decisions done during the blizzard helps readers to gain understanding applicable to many emergency situations, from natural catastrophes to man-made crises.

Readers of this book will acquire more than simply a gripping genuine account of survival. They will learn useful skills in urban disaster readiness, winter survival strategies, and the value of community in crisis events. The story also offers better knowledge of the psychological difficulties experienced during major events and techniques for preserving mental resilience under duress.

Moreover, even in apparently safe metropolitan settings, readers will grow more value for the strength of nature and the need of honoring and getting ready for her energies. The book questions accepted wisdom on the dependability of contemporary infrastructure and promotes a more proactive attitude to personal and communal safety.

As seen through the prism of a crisis, "Blizzard in Khimki" also provides insights on Russian society and culture. Beyond conventional travel writing, readers will learn about local customs, social dynamics, and the Russian approach to disaster management, therefore offering a distinctive cultural viewpoint.

Readers will be engross in the sober reality of surviving amid a modern metropolitan blizzard as the narrative progresses. From the first indicators of trouble to the heart-stopping events of the storm's strongest intensity, every chapter presents fresh difficulties and discoveries. Readers will be taken to the very core of the problem by the rich descriptions of the blinding snow, stinging cold, and terrible silence of a metropolis brought to a stop.

The story doesn't hold back on the hard facts of the circumstances. It looks at the physical effects of severe cold, the ongoing fight against hypothermia, and the difficulty to locate food and water when all usual supply lines are disrupted. Extended exposure to such severe conditions will cause readers to experience the gnawing hunger, bone-deep chill, and growing despair.

Still, among the adversity there are also times of hope, creativity, and even fun. The book honors human spirit resilience and the amazing ways in which people could adjust to even the most difficult conditions. From makeshift shelters created from urban trash to unusual friendships formed in the face of hardship, these triumphant events act as lighthouse of hope all through the story.

The book's examination of the psychological effects of a such a catastrophic occurrence is among its most intriguing features. Readers will learn about the mental difficulties experienced over protracted times of uncertainty and stress. The story explores the consequences of solitude, the fight to keep hope, and the psychological strategies applied to be motivated and concentrated when every impulse cries for submission.

Readers will also see as the narrative goes on the creation of an improvised community among the displaced people. This part of the story provides insightful teachings about leadership, teamwork, and the need of many abilities in a survival scenario. It shows how people from many backgrounds may come together to combine their knowledge and resources so raising everyone's chances of survival.

The book looks at the wider effects of such extreme weather occurrences in our changing climate in addition to the immediate survival difficulties. It begs significant issues regarding urban design, disaster readiness, and the necessity of cities to become more robust against ever erratic weather patterns.

Readers will find useful survival advice and methods artfully weaved into the storyline throughout. From techniques for melting snow for drinking water to ways of insulating temporary shelters, these ideas offer priceless information that can literally save lives in like circumstances. The book guarantees readers are both informed and entertained by carefully balancing narrative with useful knowledge.

The book also addresses the part technology plays as the crisis develops, both its advantages and constraints in dire circumstances. Readers will learn the need of having backup plans and analog abilities in an increasingly digital environment as well as how fast contemporary communication systems might collapse.

The last chapters of the book, which chronicle the storm aftermath and rescue attempts, provide a strong ending to the survival story. They provide readers a time to think back on the lessons discovered and how they could be relevant in their own life. The story keeps exploring the long-lasting effects of such a traumatic event on the survivors, their relationships, and their perspective even if the rescue marks its conclusion.

"Blizzard in Khimki: A Moscow Survival Tale" is really more than just an exciting narrative of survival against all circumstances. This is a deep investigation of human nature, a useful manual for urban disaster readiness, and a provocative analysis of our interaction with the natural world and one another. It asks readers to reflect on their own readiness for unanticipated events and fosters a greater respect of the human spirit's strength and flexibility.

Turn the pages of this book to be carried to the center of a Moscow winter storm. Experience the joys and trials of survival in one of the world's great cities brought to its knees by nature's wrath; feel the stinging cold and hear the roaring wind. Long after you have turned the last page, this narrative will linger and alter your perspective on the world and your own resilience.

Are you game to enter the blizzard? Turning the page will start the trip.

First Chapter

The sharp reminder of the quite different temperature we were walking into as we stepped foot in Moscow came from the clean winter air biting at our faces. Now, the goal of my work trip appeared nearly small as the sheer size of the Russian city overpowered my senses. Moscow, a city of great contrasts and rich history, sprang out before us, its famous onion domes dotting the skyline against a gray cloud backdrop.

But rather than the center of Moscow proper, our destination was Khimki, a satellite city just beyond the northwest perimeter of the capital. The metropolitan scene progressively gave way to a more industrial one as we moved across the busy streets. Serving as a gateway between Moscow and its international airport, Khimki, I discovered, was renowned for its aerospace sector and as a key transportation center.

Though less glitzy than central Moscow, the Khimki area has distinct appeal. Modern office buildings complemented Soviet-era apartment structures to create an architectural tapestry that chronicles Russia's tremendous growth during the previous few decades. A marvel of engineering from the Stalin era, the adjacent Moscow Canal gave the otherwise busy metropolitan setting an unexpected element of tranquilly.

I noticed the people wrapped in thick coats and fur caps as we settled into our lodging. Their clothes appeared overdone to me from what I know of milder winters. I had no idea how appreciative I would soon be of any further degree of comfort.

Wanting to know what to expect from our visit, I checked the local meteorological report. Though the accompanying images were apparent enough, the meteorologist on the television in the hotel room spoke quickly in Russian. Though nothing out of the usual for a Moscow winter, they projected a cold spell with well below freezing temperatures. Although snow was anticipated, once more this looked normal for this region of the earth.

The apparently normal forecast gave me comfort, so I redirected my focus to getting ready for the meetings that had brought me to this part of Russia. The company I represented was looking at possible joint ventures with nearby aerospace companies, and Khimki—with its concentration of industry players—was the ideal site for these conversations.

I looked out of the hotel window as I arranged my supplies and checked over my show. Since our arrival, the sky had darkened significantly; the first few snowflakes were starting to descend. The scene was bucolic, like something from a Russian tale. Youngsters in the street below pointed eagerly at the heavens, their voices barely audible through the double-glazed windows.

The delicate snowfall seemed to soften the city's rigid lines and cover the drab concrete in a covering of immaculate white. The change mesmerized me; I watched as the whirling snow and automobile headlights sliced across the deepening gloom. It was lovely, in its own right, and I let myself to savor the particular ambiance of a Russian winter evening.

Still, the snowfall got more intense as the evening dragged on. Once a light dusting, what had begun as such was rapidly turning into a heavy blanket. At times the wind picked up and drove the snow horizontally. I could feel the temperature rapidly decreasing even from the cosiness of my motel room.

Startled from my observation of the weather, a tap at my door Looked worried, it was my colleague. "Have you seen the revised forecast?" he questioned, wrinkled brow. I shook my head and reached for the remote to flip the TV on again. Now speaking more urgently, the same meteorologist from earlier was pointing to whirling patterns on the weather map behind him with furiously gestic hands.

Speaking some Russian, my colleague translated the main ideas of the report. The Moscow area was under the path of a really big winter storm, far stronger than first forecast. People were being advised by the authorities to remain indoors and get ready for possible power cuts and disturbance of transportation.

This news throws fresh light on our business strategies. Although we had meetings set for the next several days, would they even take place if the weather turned out as awful as expected? Seeking some understanding of how seriously we should treat these warnings, I grabbed for my phone to email our local friends.

I felt a twingle of excitement under my anxiety as I penned my note. Though it wasn't the vacation I had planned, it promised to be unforgettable. I had no idea how remarkable it would turn out to be.

Our local contact responded quite rapidly. Though cautious, the tone was soothing. Indeed, this area was prone to winter storms, and certainly, the infrastructure was usually ready to manage them. Still, this storm system was really big and strong. They suggested us to stock some simple items: bottled water, nonperishable food, batteries for torches just in case.

Following this counsel, my friend and I set out into the growing storm in search of a local market. Just hours ago, the streets—which had been humming with traffic—were practically empty. The handful we observed struggled against the wind and snow, heads down.

When we discovered the store, residents also following storm warnings crowded it. We managed to get some supplies and spoke using a combination of hand gestures, bad Russian, English. As outsiders, the shopkeeper—a small woman with a gentle face—seemed to grasp our situation and guided us in selecting suitable goods.

The wind howled about us as we returned to the hotel, carrying snow into every nook and corner. The few vehicles on the road proceeded slowly, their headlights hardly visible over the white mist covering all. This was not typical snowfall, it was becoming abundantly evident.

We checked notes with other guests in the lobby back in the relative safety of the hotel. Many were fellow business visitors, their plans similarly disturbed by the approaching storm. To their credit, the hotel personnel stayed cool under pressure and assured us the structure was ready for such kind of weather.

The fury of the storm grew as night fell in real force. From my chamber, I could hear the wind whistling through window frame cracks, a terrible tune emphasizing the gravity of our circumstances. The vista outside had vanished totally, replaced by a whirl of white emptiness.

That night's sleep was fitful, broken by the sounds of the storm and my own racing thoughts. Suppose the storm did not pass quickly. Suppose we were really stuck here in Khimki? Knowing that we were in a well-equipped hotel rather than in the woods helped me to calm myself; nonetheless, the sheer force of the blizzard was terrifying.

The multiple times the lights in my room flickering suggested the stress the storm was causing on the local infrastructure as the evening dragged on. I started thinking if we had done enough to get ready and mentally categorizing our supplies. In front of the wrath of nature, the business trip that had been so vital just a day ago appeared small.

The continuous white hum of the wind lulled me off to sleep in the early hours of morning. My final conscious thought was of hope for better daylight views. I had no idea that morning would bring with it a world changed and problems we had not yet imagined.

It was evident that our situation had changed from a minor weather delay into something far more dangerous as the first hints of daylight battled to break through the heavy curtain of snow. Far from fading over night, the blizzard had gotten more severe. Under feet of snow still accumulating at an alarming rate, the world beyond my window was invisible.

Second Chapter

I couldn't get rid of the impression that something was off as the sun sank on my first day in Moscow and created deep shadows across the snow-dusted streets of Khimki. The clean air that had welcomed me when I arrived had sharpened edges and a whisper of the turbulence to come. I had no idea that the next several hours would start a horrific journey that would try my toughness and endurance to the very limit.

The first hints of disaster arrived gently, practically undetectably. Once a mild friend for the day, the wind started to gather force and whistling menacingly passed between buildings. Once sloppily drifting to the ground, snowflakes now whirled with growing intensity, as if escaping an invisible attacker. I tightened my coat about me, a reflexive movement that would shortly turn into a frantic act of survival.

I first heard the word "blizzard" referenced in a quick chat with the hotel concierge. His brow wrinkled as he worked through the most recent weather report, his poor English bearing weight of concern. "Big storm coming," he added, pointing to the windows where the snow was already starting to pile at a startling rate. "Very lethal. Better still to remain indoors."

At first, the weight of his comments did not really register. Ultimately, I was a seasoned tourist used to the fluctuations in temperature around the globe. Surely, I considered, this was only a warning—the kind usually provided to visitors not conversant with local conditions. Still, I started to feel nervous in the pit of my stomach as I watched the streets outside get ever empty.

Local responses to the approaching storm combined urgent preparation with learned nonchalance. Staff members rushing to lock windows and doors caught me in a frenzy in the hotel foyer. Outside, the few still walking through the elements moved deliberately, their arms loaded with supplies and groceries. The Khimki people were obviously considering the danger seriously, their behavior louder than any kind of spoken warning could have.

The change of the scene outside my window was rather amazing as the evening progressed. Once-familiar streets had turned into foreign territory covered in a spreading white shroud. Street lamps produced ghostly halos in the gathering darkness as their light dispersed by whirling snow. Now a continual scream, the sound of the wind appeared to carry the weight of the approaching storm.

This was when my own worries started to crystallize into something more physical. The business appointments I had planned for the next day felt small in relation to the more pressing concern of guaranteeing my personal safety. A habit developed from years of travel, I found myself evaluating my resources—never before working with such haste.

prepared for a quick work trip, my bag seemed suddenly to be rather insufficient. Though definitely I had warm clothes, nothing could have survived the kind of intense cold a Russian blizzard might deliver. Food consisted just in a few snack bars and a bottle of water. Though completely charged, my phone now looked to be a flimsy connection to the outside world; its signal was already flickering as the storm grew worse.

I headed down to the little convenience store in a moment of foresight I would later be rather happy about. Though other concerned visitors and staff had already rummled over the shelves, they still housed some basics. I gathered everything I could: extra water bottles, some nonperishable food, a flashlight and batteries. His visage a mask of barely hidden anxiety, the clerk nodded favorably at my choices.

"Good decisions," he responded, with a thick but intelligible accent. "Storm like this, wondering about the duration. advisable to be ready."

His comments stayed with me as I went back to my room, arms laden with just enough food. I could not help but feel unreality as I set my supplies on the little desk. Here I was, unexpectedly getting ready for what felt like a survival situation in a sophisticated city on a typical business trip. Not least of all, the juxtaposition was startling.

Set to an English language news channel, the television in my room constantly sent updates, each more terrible than the last. Using words like "unprecedented" and "life-threatening," meteorologists, their faces dark, pointed to whirling masses of blue and white on their weather charts. They cautioned that the blizzard, which would paralyze the whole area, was looking to be among the worst in recent memory.

The whole wrath of the storm started to show itself when night fell in real force. Now howling like a living thing, the wind assaulted the windows of my room with such ferocity that I worried they would break at any minute. Driven horizontally by the breeze, the snow produced a white-out scenario that completely blocked outside visibility. The hotel seemed as though a large, furious cloud had swallowed it.

I was bouncing between pragmatic preparations and almost terror in those last hours before the storm arrived. To guard against the likelihood of pipes freezing, I checked and reexamined my supplies, charged all of my electronic equipment, and even filled the bathtub with water. Between these periods of exercise, though, I would find myself standing at the window gazing out into the maelstrom and feeling quite small and quite far from home.

I started to feel as though I was really stranded. I had nowhere to go even if I had chosen to leave. Now buried beneath a fast deepening blanket of snow, the streets were impassable. From a news update, I found that the airport had stopped all activities hours ago. For all purposes, I was imprisoned in this room, at the mercy of a storm apparently meant to bury the whole city.

The power started to flutter dangerously as the evening went on. Every brief darkness brought with it a surge of anxiety; what would happen should the electricity fail totally? The idea of being thrown into cold and darkness gave my predicament still another level of urgency. In an effort to keep some sense of control, I discovered myself mentally practicing what I would do should the worst strike. I planned every action.

The whole weight of my circumstances really came to me in these calm times, broken only by the constant howling of the wind. Alone, in a foreign nation, I was confronting perhaps historic levels of natural calamity. The business trip that had brought me here now seemed like a memory, replaced by the far more urgent needs of basic existence.

Still, I discovered I was drawing on reservoirs of power I didn't realize I had even as anxiety threatened to overtake me. Traveling for years had taught me adaptation; now, those abilities were being tested to the most extreme. I reminded myself that my best friends in this regard were meticulous planning and clear thought; panic would not help.

I slipped into a restless watch as the evening grew darker and the storm raged on. Sleep, I understood, would be harmful at worst and elusive at best. Rather, I watched the news, rationed my supplies, and just listened to the rage of the blizzard outside. Every hour that went by seemed like an eternity, yet it also seemed like a little triumph—one more hour lived, one step closer to the end of the storm.

As the storm peaked in the darkest hours of the night, my mind turned to home, to family and friends unaware of the danger I now confronted. The barrier between us, always present but rarely felt so acutely, now seemed immense and unbridgeable. I silently promised myself to phone more frequently and to treasure those relationships I had maybe taken for granted.

Though it seemed much like the night in the city covered in storms, as dawn arrived I prepared myself for what the new day would hold. The blizzard showed no signs of abating; its wrath was not lessened during the next hours. I understood that surviving not only the storm itself but also its aftermath, which was the real challenge still to come. We would be stuck for how long? Once the snow stopped falling, what difficulties might arise?

These problems occupied most of my thinking, hence I focused on the near future. The storm was far from done, and I knew the next days would try me in ways I had never been tested before. Looking out over the white emptiness Khimki had swallowed, I prepared myself for the difficulties ahead. I had no idea that the storm's wrath was only the start; the real struggle—a fight for survival in a metropolis brought to its knees by nature's might—was about to begin.

The temperature abruptly and dramatically changed as the day wore on. Starting as a gentle snowfall in the morning, the scene of Khimki was quickly whirling white. Even the most weather-hardened Muscovites were taken aback by the fury with which the snowstorm struck. In a few minutes, the wind howled with an unearthly intensity, blowing snow horizontally and lowering visibility to only a few meters.

The streets, which had been humming with bustle earlier in the day, rapidly cleared as people sought cover from the assault. Those who stayed outside discovered they were fighting the elements, leaning into the wind to keep straight. Once softly falling, the snow now stung the cheeks and hands with its frigid sharpness, carried by gale-force gusts seeming to arrive from all directions at once.

Perched at the window of my hotel room, I marveled as the familiar Khimki scene vanished from view. Just seconds ago, I had obviously seen the buildings across the street, but now they were hardly discernible silhouettes in a sea of white. The trees along the avenue bowed beneath the wind, their branches weighted down by fast accumulating snow. Nature seemed to have chosen to wipe the city from existence, dousing it in a thick, impervious white blanket.

The storm's noise was deafening. The wind screamed, rattling windows and prompting the building itself to creak and groan beneath the pressure. It did not only howl. Periodically, piercing cracks broke through the continuous roar—the sounds of limbs shattering under snow and ice. Nature exercising its strength and reminding us of our own frailty in the face of its might was a symphony of destruction.

A sense of unease started to develop in the pit of my stomach as I watched this spectacular change. There was no regular snowfall here. The sheer force and abruptness with which it had fallen upon us suggested something much more terrible. I remembered the earlier in the day weather prediction; there had been warnings of snow, undoubtedly, but nothing to indicate the apocalyptic vision now playing out before me.

My head flew back to the talks I had had with residents during the last three days. They had mentioned hard winters, naturally for Russia after all. Still, there was nothing that seemed to match what we were now going through even in their accounts of earlier hurricanes. One especially noteworthy remark from an old babushka at a nearby café returned to me: "When the snow comes in Moscow, it comes with teeth." I had grinned at what at the moment seemed to be a vibrant slice of local mythology. Now, seeing the snow blow outside, those words gained a terrifying fresh meaning.

As I saw the first indicators of infrastructure breaking beneath the weight of the storm, I started to realize how serious things were. The streetlights, which ought to have been on considering the gloom the snow brought, stayed dark. Windows that had been lit a short while before were now dark in the buildings across the street. Parts of the city were dark as it appeared the storm had cut out the power supply.

My phone buzzed with an emergency alert as though to validate my worries. In Russian and English, the warning cautioned of severe weather and recommended all inhabitants to stay indoors and get ready for perhaps long periods without other services or power. This was fast turning from a nuisance or a lovely winter view into a survival scenario.

My journalistic instincts took over, and even as I struggled to understand what it might imply for my personal safety, I found myself compiling the specifics of the calamity under development. Based on the way the wind was whirling around loose objects outside, it seemed somewhat above 100 kilometers per hour. Already gathering quicker than I had ever seen, the snowfall rate The temperature, which dropped quickly as the storm grew stronger.

I considered the goal of my trip to Moscow: a set of interviews and research for a narrative about Russian corporate behavior. Given this elemental assault, how fast those worries looked insignificant? My thoughts changed to already be thinking about how to modify my schedule, how to guarantee my personal safety, and wondering how long this storm might endure.

A especially strong gust of wind struck the structure as I stood there, hypnoticly flickering the lights in my room. The scene outside was changing. It was a sobering reminder of how flimsy our technological conveniences are in the face of natural wrath. I understood I had to move fast to get ready for what might be an arduy of years.

Steering clear of the window, I started to assess my circumstances. I had what supplies? Should the electricity go out and I find myself imprisoned in this room, how long could I last? Should the hotel have to be evacuated, what then? As the storm raged outside, these questions and more tore across my brain.

The blizzard felt almost personal, as if it had a grudge against the city and its people. It had hit with such suddenness and severity. I was both in amazement and terrified as I watched a big branch rip away from a tree and go cartwheels down the pavement. We were at the will of nature, most raw and forceful.

The knowledge of the intensity of the storm accompanied an unusual spectrum of feelings. There was anxiety, most definitely of the unknown, of being imprisoned, of the possible hazards ahead. But there was also a sort of excitement—that which results from being thrown into a remarkable circumstance. As a writer, I had always looked for unusual events and narratives that would grab readers. Now it seemed, I had wandered into what would be the lifetime narrative.

I found myself riveted to the window, unable to look away from the dramatic scene playing outside as the day drew on and the storm showed no indications of abating. The snow kept falling with unrelenting force, building up in drifts fast turning mountainous. Under the buildup, cars left on the street were fast vanishing into amorphous white lumps.

Sometimes I got peeks of other people in the buildings across the street, faces pressed against windows, staring at the storm with the same mix of awe and anxiety that I had. There was a sense of shared experience in those fleeting eye contacts, of being connected in our solitude by this great force of nature.

The ferocity of the storm remained unaltered by the last of the daylight. If anything, the coming darkness appeared to give the snow fresh vitality. Whistling through gaps and crevices, the wind discovered new voices to provide an unsettling, almost melodic accompaniment to the incessant cacophony. Captured in the beams of the few operational streetlights, the snow whirled and swirled in fascinating patterns to provide an ethereal environment.

The actual scope of the power cuts became clear as night fell. Now entire blocks of the city were dark, generating black islands in what ought to have been a sea of city lights. The few buildings still with electricity caught out like lighthouses in the storm, their windows ablaze with warm light that seemed to resist the chill and gloom all around them.

I really understood the possible length of this dilemma throughout this day to night change. There was no storm this strong that would sweep across in a few hours. Its sheer scope and intensity hinted that we might have days of this kind of temperature. This insight had shockingly broad consequences. Given its experience with hard winters, how would a city like Moscow handle a blizzard of this scope?

Third Chapter

My mind wandered to the millions of individuals living all around the metropolis that have to be realizing the same thing. How many were ready for a protracted period without electricity, maybe without heat? In such circumstances, how would emergency services run? The journalist inside me couldn't help but think about the wider consequences and the possibility for this to turn into a humanitarian disaster should the storm keep on unabated.

My room went dark while I considered these issues; the hotel eventually gave in to the power failures sweeping over the rest of the city. The abrupt loss of light was confusing; the blackness outside now reflected within. I stumbled for my phone, guiding over the now-unfamiliar territory of my room with its light. The loss of power brought home the gravity of the matter in a manner that even the visual show of the storm had not done. This was a direct threat to comfort, safety, and maybe survival, not only a magnificent exhibition of natural strength.

The storm appeared to get louder in the new darkness. Every creak of the structure, every whistle of wind across a window frame, gained fresh meaning. The darkness carried with it a greater sensation of solitude, of being blocked off from the outer world this structure offers.

I felt irony as I sat in the dark listening to the storm and thinking of the difficulties ahead. I had come to Moscow in search of corporate practices and to expose tales of human curiosity and financial wizardry. Rather, I discovered I was in the heart of a far more primordial tale: man against nature, the fight for existence against the elements.

That day's blizzard on Moscow and Khimki was more than just a weather occurrence. It was a reminder of our place in the natural world and of the thin layer of civilization we cover over the unadulterated power of nature. Knowing that this event would transform me—probably everyone else trapped in the path of the storm—as I got ready to meet whatever obstacles the next days would present. Along with snow and wind, the blizzard had brought a test of resiliency, creativity, and the human spirit.

I found myself psychologically getting ready for the next day as the night grew on and the storm kept its unrelenting attack. The instant future was unknown, full with possible hazards and difficulties. But I realized that this was only the start of a far longer narrative as I listened to the roaring wind and saw the whirling snow through my darkened window. An account of survival, of community, of the relentless human spirit against the will of nature. Now we had to learn to negotiate this new, white-out environment once the blizzard struck.

Fourth Chapter

Little did I know as we left the busy streets of Moscow behind and into the quieter suburban neighborhood of Khimki that the next few days would challenge my survival and fortitude to their absolute limits. The blizzard had struck with a severity that threw even the most weather-hardened residents off guard; now, as I found myself caught in this foreign land, the truth of my circumstances started to sink in.

My first reaction was to escape the neighborhood, to somehow find my way back to the relative security and familiarity of downtown Moscow.

As I quickly found, though, this was simpler said than done. Just hours before, the roads were clean and readily accessible; today, they were covered with a thick layer of snow that appeared to get deeper with every minute. Visibility was almost nonexistent; the whirling snow created a white wall that blocked view of more than a few feet ahead.

I tried to drive my rental car through the increasing circumstances, but it soon became clear that this was a pointless and risky effort. The wheels spun uselessly in the increasing snow, and more than once I sensed the car drift sideways, almost completely off-road. After what seemed like hours but was probably just thirty minutes of fight, I had to accept loss. Now more of a liability than an asset, the car was gently moved to what I believed was the side of the road.

Now that driving out of the storm was off-target, I focused on locating cover. As I got out of the car, the wind howled about me; the cold quickly slicing through my attire, while suitable for a business trip, was hopelessly inadequate for these Arctic-like circumstances. Trying to pick out any buildings that may provide cover, I looked over the blizzard.

Fortune grinned at me in that instant as I saw the faint silhouette of what seemed to be a little convenience shop not far from where I had been obliged to leave my car behind. Not knowing any better choices, I decided to head in that direction. As I hobbled across snow halfway up my calves, the small distance felt like a marathon; the wind threatened to throw me off balance with every stride.

When I got to the store, the door was kindly unlocked. The warm air within struck me like a hug as I opened it. The store was small but well-stocked—a trait that would prove to be rather helpful in the next few days. Middle-aged Yelena, the owner, stared at me with a mixture of surprise and worry as I staggered in covered in snow and shivered wildly.

"Добро пожаловать," she said, which I took to mean "Welcome" from the little Russian I had acquired. Her voice was friendly even though she clearly was worried. She obviously realized the seriousness of the situation developing outdoors.

I started to look around and create some basic survival plans as Yelena helped me clear the snow and handed me a steaming cup of tea. Though not perfect, the store provided cover from the snow and wind and, more importantly, food and drink. With my little Russian and her poor English, I told Yelena my circumstances as best I could; she kindly agreed to let me stay.

Getting inventory of the tools at my disposal came first. Along with some essential home supplies, bottled water, and a range of non-perishable foods, the store's shelves held Knowing that careful rationing would be absolutely vital should the storm linger for a long duration, I mentally noted them.

I then focused on making my own environment more pleasant. Yelena let me arrange a makeshift bed in a small back room the store had for storage out of some cardboard boxes and some blankets she had on hand.

Though it wouldn't be opulent by any means, it would offer somewhere to relax and save energy.

The day stretched on and the storm showed no indications of abating, so I started thinking about longer-term survival plans. A major issue was communication; my cell phone lost signal soon after the storm struck, isolating me from the outer world. Searching the store for a landline, I hoped to at least let someone know where I was or call emergency services, but I came nowhere.

To put it mildly, the dearth of communication choices was troubling. Being abruptly cut off from all kinds of interaction was a startling experience in our linked world. Surrounded by the roaring blizzard, it struck home the truth of exactly how isolated we had grown in our little shop in Khimki.

The temperature dropped still more as night started to set. Although working, the store's heating system battled to keep up with the very cold outside. To keep warm and to stifle the mounting worry that threatened to overtake me, I discovered I was always moving, pacing the little area.

Seeing my discomfort, Yelena tried to divert me with chat. Her cool head and sporadic smile gave a much-needed personal connection even with our linguistic barrier. As best we could, we related stories that combined simple words, gestures, and the universal language of human empathy to piece together meaning.

I couldn't help but consider the unusual paths life can follow while we spoke. Just days previously, I had been in my office back home getting ready for what seemed to be a standard business trip to Moscow. Now I was stuck in a tiny shop in Khimki, depending on the goodwill of a stranger and my own humor to make it through a blizzard of hitherto unheard-of strength.

The evening passed, and sleep proved elusive. One continual reminder of our hazardous predicament came from the howling of the wind outside. The storm muffled all other sounds, but I could find myself trying to hear any indicators of rescue vehicles or emergency services.

I could hear the edifice creaking and groaning under the weight of the mounting snow in the still times between blasts of wind. It was a disturbing sound, a reminder of the enormous powers of nature working just outside our precarious refuge.

My mind ran with ideas of home, of the family and friends who would be worried about me as I lay on my improvised bed, attempting to find a pleasant posture on the hard floor. I questioned whether they knew I was stranded in the heart of the blizzard and if news of it had got to them. My mind was much troubled by my incapacity to reassure them of my safety.

Though I was uncomfortable and worried, I made myself relax as much as I could. I understood that in the next days, especially if the storm kept raging, saving energy would be absolutely vital. The sounds of the storm and the sporadic impulse to get up and move around to fight off the chill that seemed to permeate into my very bones broke through fitful spurts of sleep.

I got up as the first light of dawn started to slink through the store's frosted windows; I felt stiff and uncomfortable but glad to have made it through the evening. The storm outside showed no indication of abating, and I knew that today would provide fresh difficulties.

Yelena was already awake, boiling water for tea on a little camping stove she had created from some back room space in the store. The sight of the steaming cups and the aroma of the making tea gave our unusual situation some little but welcome normalcy.

Yelena and I started talking about our day agenda while we sipped our tea and bit some dry crackers. Our food and water supplies had to be evaluated first; we also had to figure out how to stay warm and, if at all feasible, try to establish some kind of contact with the outside world.

Inventorying our supplies took depressing effort. Although the store was fully equipped for regular business, the idea of a protracted period of solitude made every thing valuable. We meticulously counted and arranged everything to create a rationing schedule meant to last until aid arrived or the storm passed.

Maintaining warmth turned out to be a harder problem. Although the heating system of the store was malfunctioning, we both understood that our circumstances would rapidly become severe should the power collapse. Using cardboard and newspapers to block drafts and save heat, we set about building more insulation where we could.

The day went on and we developed a kind of pattern. We watched the windows for any indication of rescue or other stranded people who could want assistance in turn. We carefully rationed our food, allowing ourselves little, frequent meals to help retain body heat and vitality. Anything to take our minds off the raging storm outside and the uncertainty of our circumstances, we tried to divert ourselves between these chores with chat and simple games.

One ongoing cause of concern was not interacting with the outside world. I discovered myself constantly checking my phone, wishing against hope that a signal may suddenly show up. Every time the "No Service" warning looked back at me, it was a sobering reminder of our isolation.

Another night drew in, accompanied by declining temperatures and a strengthening of the storm, and I started to question how long we may be able to hold out in our small haven. The blizzard appeared to be a white abyss swallowing the planet outside our windows. It felt limitless. Still, I sensed hope as I studied Yelena's resolute expression. We had lived so far, and maybe united we could face any obstacle the next days could present.

Our little shop in Khimki had evolved from a cover from the elements to a monument to human resiliency and the strength of group efforts against hardship. I was appreciative of this unanticipated survival and human connection lesson as I got ready for yet another night of uncertainty.

Outside the wind kept roaring, a continual reminder of the force of the snow. Still, a calm will had seized our small haven. Although we were stuck, we were not demoralized. We had hope as long as we possessed cover, food, and each other's company. And in that instant, hope was the most valuable tool available—huddled in a tiny shop in Khimki.

My thoughts drifted to the difficulties ahead as we relaxed in for another protracted night. The storm showed no indications of abating, and I realized our survival would rely on our capacity to adjust to this hard new reality. I had no idea, though, that the next days would challenge not only our physical stamina but also our mental fortitude in yet unthinkable ways. The real test of survival was still to come, and I couldn't help but worry what fresh difficulties the dawn would present as I floated off into a restless sleep.

Five Chapter

We now focus on nouraging our bodies for the day ahead as we move from the high-intensity exercises covered in the last chapter. Chapter 5 emphasizes fast and healthy breakfast ideas that can be made in a flash to make sure even the busiest people can start their day with a wholesome meal.

Variations of overnight oats have grown somewhat popular recently with good cause. Along with saving morning time, this flexible breakfast choice offers a filling and nutritious meal to start your day. Overnight oats are just rolled oats mixed with your preferred liquid—such as milk, almond milk, or yogurt—then left overnight in the refrigerator. The oats will have absorbed the liquid by morning, producing a creamy and mouthwatering breakfast free of cooking necessary.

Overnight oats are one of the biggest benefits in terms of their flexibility in flavors and nutritional demand. Try blending rolled oats with milk, a little honey, and some cinnamon for a classic taste profile. Top with sliced bananas and some chopped nuts in the morning for more texture and nutrients. For those looking for a protein boost, think about including a scoop of your preferred protein powder into the mix. For a creamy, fruish breakfast that will keep you full until lunch, a vanilla-flavored protein powder goes nicely with berries and a dollop of Greek yogurt.

Try a chocolate-peanut butter variant for a more decadent but still nutrient-dense choice. Along with a splash of maple syrup for sweetness, toss cocoa powder and a tablespoon of peanut butter into your oats. Top with sliced strawberries in the morning for a breakfast that seems like a treat but yet supplies necessary nutrients to start your day. "Overnight oats are an excellent way to ensure you're getting a balance of complex carbohydrates, protein, and healthy fats in your breakfast, which can help stabilize blood sugar levels and provide sustained energy throughout the morning," explains nutritionist Dr. Lisa Young.

Although overnight oats are a handy make-ahead choice, occasionally you might want a breakfast ready and enjoyed in a few minutes. Smoothies loaded with proteins come in really handy here. An outstanding approach to cram a range of nutrients into a quick, portable meal is with smoothies. Ensuring a balance of protein, good fats, and fiber will help you to make a pleasing smoothie that will keep you satisfied until your next meal.

Start with a base of your chosen liquid—water, milk, or a plant-based substitute like almond or oat milk. Then add a protein source. For a vegan, this might be a scoop of protein powder, Greek yogurt, or even silken tofu. For good fats, think about sprinkling chia seeds, a quarter of an avocado, or a spoonful of nut butter. These fats will prolong feelings of fullness and aid in slower digestion. At last add your fruits and vegetables. Smoothies especially benefit from frozen fruits since they produce a rich, creamy texture without calling for ice.

A traditional green smoothie would call for spinach, banana, pineapple, and a sloshful of vanilla protein powder. This is a great approach to include more greens into your diet since the sweetness of the fruits covers the taste of the spinach. Try mixing chocolate protein powder with frozen banana, a spoonful of almond butter, and a handful of spinach for a more dessert-like choice still loaded with nutrients. The end effect is a smoothie that tastes like a milkshake yet offers a well-balanced blend of nutrients to kick start your day.

Starting director of Yale University's Prevention Research Center, Dr. David Katz stresses the need of adding protein in breakfast: "Protein at breakfast helps with fullness throughout the morning and can minimize overeating later in the day. Maintaining energy levels and concentration depends on blood sugar, hence a breakfast high in proteins also helps stabilize it.

Make-ahead breakfast sandwiches can be a game-changer for people who still need something quick and portable but want a more conventional morning. Over the weekend, these can be made in quantities; on hectic mornings, they can be reheated rapidly. For a healthy supply of complicated carbohydrates, start with whole grain English muffins or bagel thins. Add a source of protein—turkey bacon, scrambled eggs, or a veggie sausage patty. Add a slice of cheese and some veggies like sliced tomato for a further healthy kick.

As usual, construct a batch of these sandwiches; then, wrap each one separately in parchment paper or aluminum foil. Stow them in the freezer in a big freezer bag. Just unweat a sandwich in the morning and microwave it for roughly one minute, or until heated through. The end effect is a hot, filling breakfast considerably more healthful than any fast-food choice.

Think of preparing a batch of breakfast burritos as a variation on the classic breakfast sandwich. Stuff scrambled eggs, black beans, sautéed peppers and onions, and cheese among big whole wheat tortillas. Tightly roll them; wrap in foil; freeze. For a crispier texture, reheat these in a toaster oven; else, microwave them.

Toby Amidor, a registered dietitian, stresses the need of including several food groups in your breakfast: "A healthy breakfast should include whole grains for energy, lean protein for satiety, and fruits or vegetables for vitamins, minerals, and fiber. Even on he busiest mornings, make-ahead breakfast sandwiches or burritos are a great approach to guarantee you're obtaining this balance.

If you want a sweeter beginning for the day, think about making a batch of homemade energy balls or granola bars. Made on a basis of oats, nuts, and dried fruits, they hold together with honey or maple syrup. For more taste and nutrients, toss in your preferred mix-ins—pumpkins seeds, coconut flakes, or chocolate chips. For those mornings when even a few minutes of preparation time isn't available, they offer a grab-and-go alternative and keep in the refrigerator for up to a week.

Though these quick breakfast ideas are meant for hectic schedules, nutrition shouldn't be sacrificed. Carbohydrates for energy, protein for satiety and muscle maintenance, and good fats for hormone balance and nutrition absorption each of these concepts offers a balance of macronutrients. Through the addition of fruits, vegetables, and fortified goods, they also provide chances to incorporate vital micronutrients.

"Starting your day with a nutritious breakfast sets the tone for healthier eating throughout the day," board-certified physician nutrition specialist Dr. Melina Jampolis emphasizes on the need of not skipping breakfast. It can help control your appetite, increase focus and output, and perhaps even help with weight control. The secret is to identify fast, simple choices you enjoy and that match your way of life."

As we wrap up our research on quick and healthy breakfast ideas, it's evident that, regardless of how hectic your schedule may be, you can have a healthy start to your day with some preparation and imagination. There are choices to fit every taste and time limit whether your preferred convenience is overnight oats, the rapid blend of a protein-packed smoothie, or the gratifying bite of a make-ahead breakfast sandwich. We will discuss how to sustain this good momentum throughout the day with quick and nutrient-dense lunchtime meals that can be readily packed for work or school as we enter the following chapter.

Sixth Chapter

The whole power of the blizzard had enveloped Khimki as we started Chapter 6: Navigating the White-Out, changing the once-familiar environment into a strange, dangerous one. Our first refuge's relative safety had turned into a two-edged blade, shielding us from the weather but also confining us in a perilous position with limited means. Though urgency propelled us on into the screaming white abyss, the choice to walk out into the storm was not taken lightly.

The entire violence of the storm hit our senses the instant we left the house. One relentless force, the wind seemed to be pushing on us from all sides at once. More like small shards of ice, snowflakes stung precisely across our faces. Visibility became just inches, the world beyond an unbroken wall of whirling white. The usual streets of Khimki were disappeared, replaced by undulating drifts of snow that covered all monuments and made every step a possible trip hazard.

With each person connected to the next by a homemade rope made from ripped clothes, our little group progressed slowly. Our only hope against separating in the terrible storm was this flimsy lifeline. We stopped every few feet to recalibrate ourselves with the compass we now most valued. We aimed to go to Khimki's center, where we hoped to locate more significant cover and maybe other survivors who would help with our predicament.

Though barely a few kilometers away, the trip felt like an expedition over a frigid wilderness. Under the white-out circumstances, time had no value. Minutes turned into hours as we battled the weather; every stride forward was a minor triumph against the efforts of the storm to pull us back. The cold permeated through our layers of clothes, numbing sensations and distorting judgment. We initially met our fellow survivors during one of our little breaks, curled against the wind.

Emerging from the white-out like apparitions, two figures so entrained with snow and ice seemed more yeti than human. The conference was a mix of relief and caution; in such desperate circumstances, desperation might turn even the most civilized individual into a threat. But our common situation soon promoted friendship. Locally, a married couple caught in the storm trying to get to their daughter's house Even although the storm had made most of the scenery unidentifiable, their familiarity of the area proved priceless.

Aiming for a community facility they thought would provide better cover, we veered slightly with our new friends. The trip went on, now interspersed with shouting exchanges as we discussed our scant knowledge of the storm or our circumstances. Though brief and scattered, these conversations kept our spirits high and our brains clear against the numbing cold and confusion.

The risks in our circumstances were more clear as we continued. More than once, a group member tripped into a snow-concealed obstruction or partially vanished into a drift and needed the others' combined efforts to extract him. Far from steady, the wind came in strong gusts that may have knocked us flat. I stumbled and felt myself being pulled over the snow during one very strong blast. I believed the storm would claim me for a terrible moment, but the homemade rope held strong and my friends swiftly drew me back to safety.

Only the psychological strain matched the physical toll of negotiating the storm. Our will was eroded by the wind's relentless howl, the disorienting white-out, and the gnawing uncertainty of our fate. Discussions dropped in frequency, replaced by a gloomy will to just keep going. Every one of us withdrew into our own thoughts, concentrating on the next breath, action, anything to take our minds off the severity of our circumstances.

Our most terrifying obstacle so came during one of these silent moments. Suddenly the earth under our feet changed, and we gasped together knowing we had stumbled upon the frozen surface of a little lake or pond. Fortunately thick enough to sustain our weight, the ice moaned and crested with every stride. The knowledge of how readily we could have dropped into cold water made me shiver, unrelated to the weather.

We gently, with painful slowness, moved across the rink. Every crack and change drove surges of adrenaline through our tired bodies. It was a sobering reminder of how the storm had turned the known terrain of Khimki into a dangerous obstacle course. Once securely across, we stopped more than usual and each of us silently considered the nearly catastrophic event we had just negotiated.

A small glow started to pierce the white-out as we started again. I first discounted it as a trick of the light or maybe a hallucination brought on by tiredness. But the glow changed to become the warm yellow light of windows as we approached. We arrived at the community center, a strong, three-story structure amid the storm-torn terrain that offered hope.

The relief of having cover was unbounded. The relative warmth of the interior and the abrupt lack of breeze as we staggered across the doors assaulted us like a physical force. Filled with other storm migrants, the community center had evolved into a temporary emergency shelter. After our ordeal, seeing other survivors and hearing human voices not muffled by howling wind seemed nearly strange.

Those already there stirred with our arrival. We were bombarded with queries about conditions outside and whether we had seen any evidence of rescue attempts as we dropped our snow-encrusted outer clothes. We discovered later that although the facility had some emergency supplies—food and blankets—communication with the outside world remained cut off. We were informed the storm had exceeded all forecasts and caught even the most ready authorities off guard.

I considered our dangerous trip over the white-out as we relaxed into the relative security of the community center. The encounter had stretched us intellectually as much as physically. Still, it had also shown the amazing fortitude of the human spirit and the force of group effort against hardship. Stranger forced together by circumstance, our tiny group had bonded in the furnace of survival.

Though the community center offered a brief respite, we all realized our ordeal was far from finished. The storm raged outside, and the difficulties of life in a city crippled by the blizzard were only starting to play out. I pondered what fresh challenges the next days would bring and whether the fragile protection we had discovered would be sufficient to see us through as I listened to the wind slamming against the building.

The community center's mood changed as evening descended. The first solace from seeking cover gave way to a mounting concern about the future. Many of those assembled had family members elsewhere in the city, and the lack of communication exacerbated fears. Discussions shifted to conjecture on the duration of the storm and the possible aftermath. For many, like me, sleep remained elusive even in the cosiness and relative comfort of our surrounds.

Under the low light of emergency lamps, I watched the varied gathering of people brought together by the blizzard. Families with small children, senior couples, and single people like me were among them. Some gathered in small groups to tell stories and console one another. Others sat by themselves, buried in their own thoughts. Although everyone was clearly under stress from the circumstances, the common experience of surviving had produced an instant community.

I was chatting with a local teacher called Yelena late into the evening. She expressed worries about her students, many of whom resided in Khimki's outer neighborhoods. Her voice a mix of astonishment and concern, she remarked, "In all my years here, I have never seen a storm like this."

"I worry especially for the elderly and the sick people who might be imprisoned in their homes." Her remarks highlighted the scope of the catastrophe and the several unsung tales of struggle and survival taking place all around the city.

The morning that followed offered no relief from the tempest. If anything, it seemed to have got more intense over night. Snow totally covered the community center's windows, and the structure creased under the attack of the wind. Our realization of the whole degree of our isolation destroyed any chances of a rapid rescue.

The difficulties of our circumstances emerged as the day went on. Although at first seeming plenty, the center's emergency supplies were obviously not meant to last for such a sizable gathering for very long. Rationing turned into a demand that resulted in heated debates and the need of a just distribution system. It was a sobering reminder of how rapidly, in the face of shortage, society conventions may collapse.

Notwithstanding the challenges, flashes of warmth and generosity emerged. I observed as strangers offered what little they had, calmed young children, and cooperated to make our sanctuary as pleasant as could be. These incredibly poignant deeds of kindness under hardship were evidence of the human spirit's resiliency.

Our predicament in the community center stays unstable as we near the end of this chapter. The storm shows no signs of stopping, and the difficulties of survival in this remote location are just starting to surface. Our shared situation has deepened the relationships created during our dangerous trip across the white-out; but, they will surely be tested in the next days.

Anticipating the next chapter, we will discuss the developing problem with communication breakdown. The isolation of our circumstances gets increasingly evident when phone signals falter and internet connections vanish. Being cut off from the outside world and coupled with the physical obstacles of our surroundings will drive us to our boundaries psychologically. We shall explore the several attempts to get emergency services as well as the mounting desperation resulting from their fruitfulness. The chapter will also look at how this lack of communication influences the group dynamics in our improvised shelter since gossip and speculation occupy the hole left by concrete knowledge.

Seventh Chapter

Moving from the difficulties negotiating the white-out circumstances, we now face an equally difficult barrier: total breakdown of communication. Apart from covering Khimki with a heavy coating of snow, the storm had destroyed our lifelines to the outside world. We were plunged into an isolation as deep as it was surprising when phone signal and internet connection vanished.

Our communication breakdown surfaced slowly at first. It originally appeared to be a momentary problem, the kind of sporadic service interruption one would have during bad weather. With fingers numb from cold, I remember pulling out my phone hoping to check for updates on the storm or communicate to my colleagues back home. The "No Service" light pointed back at me, a menacing forerunner of the difficulties to come.

Hours went by and the weight of our circumstances grew more clear-cut. In a time when we consider continuous connectivity as second nature, the abrupt lack of this modern ease was startling. It was about being deprived of essential knowledge and possible rescue operations, not only about not being able to check emails or browse social media. The storm had carried us back to a pre-digital age, in which our local surroundings comprised our whole planet.

Efforts at getting emergency services came up short. Every missed call served as a reminder of our frailty. The emergency numbers we had been taught to depend on were now simply meaningless digits. Realizing that the raw power of nature could make the complex networks we rely on outdated, was a humble experience. One other stranded visitor said, "It's like we've been thrown back in time." None Google, none GPS, nothing at all. We live for ourselves.

This communication breakdown caused great psychological impact by isolating people. Human beings are social creatures, hence the abrupt cut off of our capacity to interact with loved ones or consult authorities resulted in a clear sensation of anxiousness. I watched how this affected the people who were stuck with me as well as myself. Some started to get impatient, repeatedly looking for a signal on useless phones. Others seemed to turn inward, maybe as a coping strategy against the intense aloneness.

Although I have frequently written as a journalist on the psychological consequences of solitude, personally living under such extreme conditions was quite different. Our digital devices' solitude reflected the terrible quiet of the storm-torn countryside outside. It magnified every concern, every doubt about our future. Would contribute come? Not one person even knew we were here. These questions spun constantly in our brains without any solutions showing up.

Furthermore encouraged by ignorance were rumors and supposition. We were left to evaluate the matter depending on our few observations without access to official weather forecasts or news updates. Every shift in the strength of the wind or a little pause in the snowfall became the focus of much debate and often somewhat different conclusions. While some felt the storm was just building power for another assault, others sensed it was abating. This knowledge vacuum compounded the tension already present in a difficult circumstance.

Some of us started looking at more conventional means of calling for aid in an effort to close this communication gap. We talked about the likelihood of building big SOS signs in the snow that would be seen from the air should rescue helicopters fly over. Others advised attracting possible rescuers using mirrors or any reflecting surface. Though maybe out of date in our often hyper-connected society, these principles now promised redemption.

The encounter made clear how brittle our current communication system is. An IT specialist among my fellow stranded people noted, "We've created these incredible networks, but they're still vulnerable to extreme weather. It's a wake-up call on our increasing reliance on technology. This realization sparked debates on the necessity of more strong, weather-resistant communication networks, particularly in places vulnerable to frequent storms.

The absence of communication started to mold our behavior and decision-making process as the hours turned into days. We had to rely on our own judgment and communal wisdom without the capacity to call for direction or help. This compelled self-reliance was terrible as well as inspiring. It motivated us, on the one hand, to be more determined and creative. Conversely, it made every choice more weighty since, should something go wrong, we cannot readily consult counsel or assistance.

Our sense of time suffered as well from the communication breakdown. Our sense of hours and days started to blur without the continual pings of notifications or the internet time check capability. We discovered that our hunger cycles, the shifting light, the rhythms of the storm outside, were our more fundamental means of timekeeping. This disturbance of our usual temporal anchors fit the bizarre character of our circumstances.

The difficulty to convince loved ones of our safety was among the most demanding features of this communication hole. The idea of my family worried about my location and well-being is intolerable as a parent and husband. I was writing mental messages to them, pledges of return and declarations of love, hoping that somehow, via some mysterious link, they would realize that I was alive and battling to return.

The encounter also sharpened the value of human-to—human communication. We discovered that we were interacting more directly and deeply with each other without our smartphones to moderate our exchanges. Talks that would have been cursory under normal conditions become lifelines of support and company. We told tales, worries, and hopes that would have been unusual in our typically technologically-saturated existence. We bonded over these things.

As we worked through this forced digital detox, some discovered unanticipated advantages. One Moscow-based marketing executive thought, "It's terrible, certainly, but being disconnected also has freeing powers. I'm not always checking my phone, first of all in years. Even though this is a terrifying moment, I am totally present right now. Many of us could relate to her comments, which underlined the two-edged character of our regular contact.

The breakdown of communication also made us rediscover and depend on more conventional kinds of amusement and time-passing. Someone discovered a deck of cards, which spurred unofficial competitions meant to maintain morale. Others turned to narrative, relating novels they had read or stories from their own life. These analog kinds of involvement promoted a feeling of community that might not have grown otherwise free from the continual interruptions of notifications and updates.

Our primary obstacle as we neared what we anticipated to be the end of our adventure was still lack of communication. Everyone carried great weight on the uncertainty of when or whether aid would arrive. We had no idea whether search teams had been set up, whether our absence had been observed, or whether the outside world even realized the whole degree of the storm's effects on Khimki.

All of us were permanently changed by this period of mandated silence and solitude. It made us face our own ingenuity and resilience and questioned our presumptions about the dependability of modern technologies. As we would subsequently learn, our experience was not unusual. Affecting thousands of people and complicating rescue attempts, the storm had caused extensive communication failures over the whole area.

As we kept negotiating the difficulties presented by the blizzard, the lessons acquired from this communication breakdown would be useful in the next days. Maintaining our morale and organizing our group efforts for survival and final rescue would depend critically on our capacity to adjust to this abrupt separation from the digital world.

We started to concentrate more closely on the near difficulties of survival as the howling winds outside carried with them the solitude of our digital quiet. Our main concern became the need to protect our shelter and acquire basic needs, so guiding the aggravation of our communication breakdown to the background. Little did we know that as we entered the following stage of our journey—the evolution of survival skills vital for surviving the continuous storm—this forced self-reliance and the relationships created in silence would soon be tested.

Eighth Chapter

Examining the nuances of survival strategies helps us to see that, in times of crisis, human ability for creativity and adaptation is usually at its best. The blizzard that had overtaken Khimki had driven us all to our limits and compelled us to draw on hitherto unrealized sources of creativity.

Focusing on three primary areas—improved tools and equipment, food and water management, and keeping body heat in extreme cold—this chapter will examine the several ways and techniques used to endure the difficult circumstances.

Our first line of protection against the unrelenting storm became the skill of improvisation. We had to turn commonplace items into life-saving instruments with few resources at our hand. Our creation of a makeshift snow shovel was among the most important objects we produced. We made a contraption that let us clear snow from doors and build windbreaks using the flat side of a suitcase and fastening it to a broken broom handle with a belt. This apparently basic tool proved quite helpful in our attempts to keep some degree of control over our immediate surroundings.

An other crucial makeshift equipment was a signaling gadget. We disassembled a side mirror from a car and fashioned a crude heliograph from the reflecting surface. For most of our trip, the thick cloud cover made it useless; but, we kept it available in case a break in the weather might let us signal for assistance. As survival guru Bear Grylls once observed, "improvisation is the secret to survival. You never know what you will have at hand, hence you must be ready to make use of everything and anything to your benefit."

Apart from tools, we also had to create makeshift safety clothing. Having come to Moscow for business instead of arctic exploration, many of us were unprepared for the degree of the blizzard. To keep snow out of our shoes, we pulled plastic bags over them and tied them at the ankle like improvised gaiters. Newspapers were piled between layers of clothing to act as extra insulation. These basic changes greatly improved our capacity to resist the severe cold and wind.

One of the more creative improvisations came in the form of a snow melting gadget. We built a little stove from an empty metal container by drilling holes close to the bottom for airflow and cutting a bigger hole in the top. Fuel consisted on little bits of wood and paper; snow piled on top would melt and provide a consistent, if limited, supply of water. This tool became key to our water management plan, which was very vital for our existence.

In a winter survival situation, water management offers special difficulties. Surrounded with snow and ice, we ironically ran the danger of dehydration. The dry, cold air raised our bodies' water needs; the energy used to melt snow for drink taxed our meager resources. We set up a rapid schedule of gathering and melting snow so that everyone would have water all through the day.

We designed a technique whereby snow was first packed into containers and hauled inside our shelter in order to maximize efficiency and fuel economy. The somewhat higher inside temperature would start the melting process, therefore saving some energy required to completely liquefy the snow. We also discovered that eating snow straight will reduce our core body temperature and demand more energy to melt in our stomachs.

Food management evolved as still another vital component of our survival plan. Rationing was crucial even though we had no idea how long we would be stuck. We compiled a common supply by pooling our resources after inventory of all the food sources we could find. Items many had brought as trip snacks—energy-dense foods like almonds, chocolate bars, and dried fruits—became valuable goods.

We instituted a rigorous rationing program, distributing tiny amounts throughout day to keep energy levels high and raise spirits. Meal times evolved into ritualistic events that gave our days organization and a feeling of normalcy in an otherwise turbulent environment. We also observed that warm meals, even in tiny amounts, greatly improved our emotional and bodily states. We made basic soups that felt like feasts in our desperate circumstances and heated canned items using our makeshift stove.

Another element of our approach to food management included foraging. Although the blizzard made travel risky from our refuge, we searched the nearby area for any possible food supplies. Although urban foraging in a winter storm is far from perfect, we were able to locate several edible plants peeking through the snow and even some frozen berries, albeit not very nutritional, gave our limited diet psychological boost and diversity.

Perhaps the most important and ongoing difficulty we encountered was keeping body heat in severe weather. Though the human body is quite strong, continuous exposure to low temperatures can cause hypothermia and frostbite very rapidly. Our first line of protection was appropriate wardrobe arrangement. Instead of a few thick layers, we used the numerous thin layer concept to improve insulation and enable layer addition or removal as necessary temperature control.

Our first focus became building a good cover inside our current construction. We created a tiny enclosed space inside the bigger building using furniture, drapes, and whatever materials were at hand. This "room inside a room" idea let us focus our body heat in a more controllable space. We also used the buddy system, matching off to distribute body heat at rest intervals. This warmed us and let us keep an eye on one another for hypothermia symptoms.

Our survival benefited from both physical exercise and its opposite. Movement produced body heat and, on one hand, served to keep circulation intact. Conversely, too much perspiration might cause our clothes to get wet, which would rapidly freeze and speed up heat loss. Stretches, isometric workouts, and even basic dancing motions were part of our regimen of controlled activities fit for our limited space. These exercises maintained our blood flow without causing undue effort.

One especially successful method we used was making "heat bottles." Hot water from our snow-melting activity filled water bottles, which we positioned deliberately throughout our bodies—especially near important arteries in the neck, armpits, and crotch. During the coldest times, this approach helped us to keep our core temperature and supplied localized heat.

We started to realize the great truth in the words of adventurer Aron Ralston: "You don't have to be an expert to survive; you just have to be determined." As we put these survival strategies into use Our battle against the merciless elements was built mostly on our will and on these makeshift tactics.

Though they were formed out of need, the skills we learned and polished during our ordeal in Khimki taught us important lessons about human resiliency and adaptation. Looking ahead to the development of a larger community of survivors in the next chapter, it is evident that these abilities and the attitude they promoted would be rather helpful in our group efforts to survive and finally overcome the blizzard that had so profoundly changed our lives.

Ninth Chapter

As we negotiated the unrelenting snowfall covering Khimki, an amazing phenomena started to develop. The terrible circumstances endangering our very survival also acted as impetus for the birth of an improvised society. This surprising bright side in our terrible circumstances would show to be absolutely vital for our group fight against the elements.

Banding together among other survivors was both natural and required. We started to come across additional trapped people and small groups when sight cleared somewhat during occasional storm lulls. Every face we encountered reflected the same sense of hope and relief at seeing other people in this great white canvas. Our little shelter started to become a hive of activity and shared determination as our instinct to pull together in the face of difficulty took over.

Alexei, a local factory worker caught in the storm on his way home from his night shift, joined our group among the first. His familiarity of the neighborhood was quite helpful since he could lead others to our improvised haven. Marina, a school teacher who had been stuck in her car with her adolescent son Ivan, trailed closely behind him. Their arrival signaled a sea change in our group's collective morale since Ivan's young vitality and Marina's cool headiness injected a much-needed dose of hope into us.

Our numbers increased along with the wealth of knowledge and tools at our hands. Every new newcomer carried not just their belongings but also their own special talents and background. Retired military officer Dmitry took care of setting up our refuge and creating a watch system. His years of survival-oriented training turned out to be our biggest advantage since he provided methods for controlling our little resources and saving heat.

The distribution of resources turned into pillar of our just established society. While some people donated warm clothing or tools they had managed to recover from their cars, others ate food voluntarily split among the group. Olga, an elderly woman who had been saved from her apartment by two young guys, was maybe the epitome of this kind of giving. She insisted on sharing the homemade preserves she had packed, despite her own frailty, saying resolutely, "We will all get through this together or not at all."

Sharing knowledge became just as vital as tangible resources. Every one of our group members had unique knowledge. Enthusiastic about the wildness, Nikolai showed us how to manufacture temporary snow goggles from whatever we had on hand to guard our eyes from the blinding white terrain. Setting up a little first aid station, Yana, a nurse, gave priceless guidance on avoiding hypothermia and frostbite.

Our combined knowledge helped us to create increasingly advanced survival plans. Dmitry guided us in forming teams, each in charge of various facets of our survival. One crew concentrated on keeping our shelter intact and insulating it as best they could against the howling gusts. Another crew was in charge of our food and water supply, so closely limiting our resources to make sure they would last as long as needed.

The squad that signaled for aid was maybe the most important one. Under the direction of former radio operator Sergei, this team put out great effort to figure out how to let possible rescuers know where we were. Seeking to strengthen any weak signals that might find their way through the storm, they built temporary antennae from trash. When technological approaches failed, they resorted to more conventional ways and produced significant SOS signals in the snow using any black substance we could locate.

One cannot overstate the psychological effects of creating this community. Under such dire conditions, the human relationship we developed turned into a lifeline that helped to ward hopelessness. We spoke tales of our life, our family, and our future hopes. These talks not only helped us to escape our terrible circumstances but also improved our relationships and fostered unity among us that would be quite important in the next days.

One especially moving scene saw Anya, a young mother away from her child, crying out concern and frustration. Around her, the group came together to provide words of consolation and hope. Using her teaching skills, Marina planned a group sing-along of classic Russian folk tunes. If only momentarily, the sound of our voices rising together in unison seemed to be pushing back against the howling wind.

Our sense of solidarity was tested to the very last when darkness descended and the temperature plummeted much further. We gathered for warmth and alternated naps while others kept watch. The real power of our makeshift family emerged in these calm times while the storm raged outside. Days ago, strangers, we now relied on one another for survival; our destinies were tightly entwined.

Our challenges were not just physical ones. Keeping morale as hours turned into days become more challenging. These were the times when the variety of our group turned out to be our biggest advantage. Trade-based stand-up comedian Vasily volunteered to lighten the situation with jokes and funny anecdotes. His laughter, resounding in our shelter, reminded us that mankind's spirit could not be destroyed even in the worst of circumstances.

Our group's efforts to signal for aid became almost ceremonial. We would renew our efforts to interact with the outside world every hour, on the hour. We would alternately yell into the emptiness, fly homemade flags, and rekindle signal fires threatened to be extinguished by the unrelenting snow. Though usually useless, their deeds provided us hope and direction. Every effort was a protest against the storm, a vow that we would not silently yield to its rage.

Our period in seclusion started to be seen through a wider prism as it went on. Discussions shifted to the essence of community itself and how the ties we had developed during crisis reflected the best sides of human nature. The factory worker Alexei thought about how this event stood against the sometimes alienating character of modern metropolitan living. "In normal times," he said, "I hardly know my neighbors. I would now trust any of you with my life."

Others in the group also felt this way. Emphasizing the value of community resilience and cooperation, Marina, the teacher, discussed how she would include the lessons acquired from our experience into her syllabus. Even the always austere Dmitry acknowledged that the event had altered his view of citizen capacity during emergencies.

As our chapter on the founding of our impromptu society draws to a close, let us consider the transforming potential of common suffering. The snow that threatened our life also eliminated the manmade borders that sometimes divide us in daily existence. Social level, occupation, age - none of these counted in the face of our common survival fight. Instead what showed up was a pure kind of human connection grounded in common need and a will to keep on.

Every one of us would bear lifelong effects from the community we created during those terrible days. The ties developed in that temporary shelter would linger long after the snow melted and we resumed our regular routines. We had seen each other at our most vulnerable, and by doing so we found the power in togetherness.

We were confronting a different difficulty as the raging winds started to calm and the first faint signals of help showed on the horizon. Separating ourselves loomed ahead, a mixed reminder that our time together was running out. Even as we got ready to go back to our separate lives, we realized that the knowledge gained and the relationships built will always shape us long after the snowfall turned into a memory.

Tenth Chapter

A new sound cut through the roaring wind as the intensity of the blizzard started to fade: the far-off whirl of chopper rotors. For those of us who had gathered in our improvised shelter, this sound sent off both wonder and incredulity. After days of solitude, walled off from the world by walls of white, rescue was at last close. The arrival of rescue services indicated the start of a deep period of introspection and personal development as well as the conclusion of our terrible trip in Khimki.

The rescue effort provided evidence of human resiliency and emergency responder determination. The faces of men and women who had risked the aftermath of the blizzard to locate us greeted us as the chopper landed in a clearing our group had hurriedly created. Their facial expressions combined determination to bring us all to safety with relief at locating survivors. A tough man with a beard covered with frost, the lead rescuer came up to us smiling reassuringly. "You've made it," he said in strongly accented English. Let us now get you home.

The trip back to safety seemed strange. I looked down at the changed scene below as we were flown from the prison we had spent days in. Once a busy Moscow suburb, Khimki now lay buried by feet of snow. Roads had vanished, houses were little more than lumps in a sea of white, and occasionally other rescue efforts could be seen as small dots of activity over the huge snowfield. It was a sobering sight, a reminder of the great force of nature and the frailty of human infrastructure against such forces.

When we arrived at a makeshift emergency facility outside Moscow, medical personnel attended to us right away. As we were assessed for frostbite, dehydration, and other cold-related symptoms, our ordeal's physical toll became clear. Fortunately, most of us had just suffered minor injuries after working together and using the survival skills we had developed. But the psychological effect was clear in my fellow survivors' empty eyes and uneasy demeanours.

The reality of what we had gone through sank in as we started to warm up—physically and emotionally. Driven for first-hand stories of survival against all circumstances, reporters crowded the center. Arriving government officials expressed alarm and promised inquiries into the degree of preparedness—or lack—for such severe weather events. For those of us who had experienced it, though, the most crucial talks were among us.

We filled in the blanks of our common narrative by sharing our unique experiences in the still times between tests and consultations. These talks helped me to really value the knowledge gained from our stay through the blizzard. Perhaps the most startling was the value of community and teamwork under crisis. "I never thought I would depend so much on strangers," Elena, a local schoolteacher who had attended our group, stated. "But now, I cannot see surviving without all of you."

The relationships developed in the face of hardship were indeed robust. Although everyone of us had entered the storm personally—businessmen, visitors, residents—we had come out as a close-knit group. Like snow in April, the synthetic walls of social level, nationality, and background had melted away to leave only a pure, basic human connection. This, I came to see, was maybe the most important lesson our ordeal produced.

Still another vital lesson was the need of flexibility and readiness. Those of us with some rudimentary knowledge of survival skills, however, had been rather helpful in directing group activities. Gruff ex military man Igor had been especially helpful. "They teach you to respect nature in the army," he said. "But one thing to know it is; another is to live it. This event transforms you."

When I thought back on our makeshift tools and strategies for obtaining food and staying warm, I was amazed by the inventiveness born of need. We had turned commonplace objects into life-saving tools, and in doing so we had drawn on a creative reservoir most of us lacked. It was a sobering reminder of the latent abilities each of us has, often unappreciated until events drive them to the surface.

Another area of great learning was the psychological resilience needed to withstand such an event. Many of us had pushed ourselves to the brink mentally from the solitude and uncertainty. American visitor Sarah, who had been on holiday in Moscow, spoke brilliantly about this. "There were times when I wanted to give up," she said. "But then it gave me strength when I looked about at everyone else battling to survive. I discovered that the human soul is far more potent than I could have ever dreamed."

There was a clear sense of thanks mixed with incredulity as the day drew on and we started to be returned to our homes or temporary lodging. One week ago, we had survived an occurrence that would have appeared improbable. The planet we were returning to felt both familiar and alien; the daily pleasures of heated baths and cosy beds now looked like luxuries beyond measure.

As I got back into my regular life in the days and weeks that followed, I discovered minor but notable changes. The event had changed my priorities and made me more conscious of the frailty of our contemporary life and more grateful of the little pleasures in life. Respecting its strength and developing a closer relationship to the natural world, I found myself increasingly pulled to nature.

As the snow melted and spring arrived, the media focus finally dropped and life in Moscow and Khimki resumed normal. For some of us who had experienced the blizzard, though, its effects persisted. We kept in touch, our common experience forging a link that went beyond our few days together. Regular get-togethers evolved into times for introspection and celebration of life.

When I consider the whole experience—from my arrival in Moscow to the time of rescue—the path of personal development it offers really strikes me. Originally a regular business trip, what had begun as such had become a deep life lesson in resiliency, community, and the human spirit. The blizzard in Khimki had been a transforming event that had changed my perspective of myself and my role in the world, not only a physical one to conquer.

"In every walk with nature, one receives far more than he seeks," the naturalist John Muir once said, and this reminds me as I finish this narrative of our survival and rescue. Indeed, our unplanned "walk" with nature in the middle of a Russian winter had produced far more than we could have ever dreamed. It had peeled off the surface of contemporary existence and exposed the core of human power and connection that underneath.

The knowledge gained on those days spent snowbound in Khimki still shapes my life. They act as a continual reminder of the need of being ready, the power of community, and the resiliency of the human spirit. Looking ahead, both personally and globally, I take with me the understanding that even in the worst, coldest events, human connection and hope to be extracted from our natural capacity to adapt and survive.

The blizzard in Khimki told more than just a story of survival against all circumstances. It was a tale of human perseverance, creativity, and the strong ties developed in the furnace of hardship. Perhaps our experience can be both a warning and a lighthouse of hope as the globe deals with increasingly erratic climate events and natural calamities; it reminds us of the difficulties we could encounter but also of our great ability to overcome them collectively.

Book Conclusion

Making it through the blizzard in Khimki was a life-changing event that tried human fortitude and creativity to the most. From the storm's unexpected start to the horrific days that followed, this experience highlighted the erratic character of severe weather events and the need of being ready. From a standard business trip to a fight for survival, the experience highlighted the frailty of our contemporary comforts and the unvarnished might of nature.

This experience made clear the value of flexibility and creativity. In the face of difficult circumstances, improvisational skills, smart resource management, and creative survival strategies proved absolutely vital. The psychological effects of solitude and uncertainty were significant and emphasized the mental strength needed to go beyond such obstacles. These encounters remind us sharply of the requirement of mental readiness and fundamental survival skills in our ever changing environment.

The lesson on the value of community in times of crises maybe the most important one this experience taught. The gathering of a temporary group of survivors showed how strangers may unite to combine knowledge and resources, therefore raising their odds of survival. This feeling of oneness under difficulty represents the natural human ability for compassion and cooperation even in the most extreme conditions.

The rescue and later analysis give insightful analysis of emergency response and readiness. The loss of communication systems during the storm emphasizes the need of strong emergency plans and the weaknesses in our technologically dependent culture. Furthermore, the personal development attained during this crisis is evidence of the human spirit's capacity to adjust and get strength from great difficulty.

Ultimately, Khimki's blizzard serves as a potent reminder of both nature's might and human resiliency. It emphasizes the need of community, flexibility, and readiness in conquering obstacles that might kill one. The lessons from this Moscow survival story provide insightful analysis for both people and societies as we negotiate an uncertain future with rising climate-related hazards.